ORIGINS

RAISED BY 1912
BOOK 1

KISCHA NICOL HERNANDEZ

Copyright © 2026 Kischa Nicol Hernandez

All rights reserved.

No part of this book may be reproduced, distributed, or transmitted in any form or by any means, including photocopying, recording, or other electronic or mechanical methods, without the prior written permission of the publisher, except in the case of brief quotations embodied in critical reviews and certain other noncommercial uses permitted by copyright law.

This is a work of creative nonfiction. Names, places, and identifying details have been changed where appropriate to protect privacy.

First edition.

Published by Storyhouse™ Publishing

United States of America

ISBN: 979-8-9940945-2-5

For the women who held the house together when the world asked too much of them.

We inherit what is unfinished

and make a life from it.

AUTHOR'S NOTE

This book is not an attempt to explain my family.

It is an act of witness.

What follows is not a complete history, nor a full accounting of the lives that shaped mine. It is a beginning—a tracing of origins, routines, silences, and the structures that held long before I had language for them.

Raised by 1912™ is a series about inheritance: what is passed down, what is withheld, and what we are left to carry on our own. Book I exists to establish the ground. The house. The rules. The quiet.

The rest of the story unfolds from there.

LEGACY

Long before any of us knew our own names—before we had stories or memories or language—there was a man and a woman living in a world that demanded everything from them and promised almost nothing in return.

My grandparents, Hesteler Bleu and Jake Gipson, were not people of formal education or privilege. My grandmother had only a seventh-grade education and was married at fourteen. My grandfather likely did not finish high school and never stepped foot on a college campus. They were born into a time when survival was a full-time occupation and opportunity was a luxury reserved for other people.

And yet—

From that soil,

from that scarcity,

from those limitations,

they built a family that rose.

They built a house that endured.

They raised sixteen children—sixteen lives shaped by discipline, faith, routine, and the unspoken expectation that each generation should climb higher than the one before it. Four of their babies did not survive childbirth, grief my grandmother carried without ceremony or language. But the rest lived on, and from that surviving group came futures far beyond what life had prepared her to imagine.

The miracle is not simply that the children lived.

The miracle is what they became.

My grandmother birthed those children into a world with a single stove, a single washboard, and a single pair of hands. She mothered them through economic droughts and personal storms, through segregation, through loss, through the kind of exhaustion a fourteen-year-old bride could never have anticipated. She did it without complaint, without softness, and without any blueprint except the one she carved with her own two hands.

Out of that house—

the one she built with Jake,

the one she ruled with quiet authority,

the one she held together by force of will—

came sons who stepped into futures she never had access to.

The majority of their sons earned college degrees, became men of standing, men of accomplishment. Men who carried the Gipson name into rooms their parents were never allowed to enter.

There was Uncle Alvin, the eldest, now ninety-seven years old, who became Mayor of Arcola, Texas—a man who led a city with the same steadiness he learned in his mother's home. There was Uncle Alvarn, who built a ranching life in Arcola, living next door to his brother, owning land—Black landownership, a victory of its own in the South. And Uncle "Buddy" Henry—still alive, still educated, still steady.

These men were not raised by scholars. They were raised by endurance. By a mother who knew routine better than rest. By a father who worked without seeking applause. By a house that did not know luxury but understood dignity.

What Jake and Hesteler built was more than a family.

It was a trajectory.

A direction.

A foundation.

1
ARRIVAL INTO A WORLD ALREADY LIVING

I arrived in the late 1970s to a house that had already lived enough for all of us. Nothing in it was becoming anything new. The routines were established, the land had been claimed, the flower beds had long since learned the shape of my grandmother's hands. The noise of raising sixteen children had quieted into a steady hum, and the house had settled into itself the way older women do—no longer loud, no longer proving, just present.

I did not enter a beginning.

I entered a life already in motion.

The house did not shift itself because I arrived.

It absorbed me.

From my earliest days, mornings began before I understood what time was. Sunrise did not wake my grandmother—she woke the sunrise. Her feet touched the floor with the certainty of someone who had done this for decades, someone who knew exactly what the day required. By the time the rest of us stirred, she had already moved through the quiet, her steps steady, her breath unhurried.

Some mornings I woke before she did, though I didn't know it at the time. I would lie still, watching the light creep across the wall, waiting for the familiar sounds to begin. When they did—the strike of a match, the clatter of a pan—I felt something loosen in my chest. The day had begun correctly. We were safe inside it.

The kitchen came alive without ceremony.

A match struck.

Blue flame softened into gold.

The cast-iron skillet waited on its rightful eye, seasoned by years of feeding generations that would have gone hungry without her hands. Coffee percolated on the back burner. Bacon popped, pulling the house awake whether anyone wanted to rise or not. Biscuits were made from scratch—no shortcuts, no cans—her fingers moving with a memory older than I was.

Breakfast was never just a meal. It was proof that the house, and everyone in it, was anchored.

The table was set the same way every morning: simple plates, folded napkins, butter churned by her own hands. There was order even in the smallest things—not an order that pressed down on you, but one that steadied you.

Outside, the chickens rustled in the yard, waiting for her steps. She fed them first, as if acknowledging their role in the morning's work. They trusted her voice, her presence, her patience. She moved among them with a calm that made even the birds settle.

This was the world I grew up inside—quiet, sure, unfolding each day the same without ever feeling dull. The rhythm steadied the bones of the house and everyone sheltered inside it. She did not need to speak for the house to feel alive. She did not need to say she loved us; the biscuits said it, the eggs said it, the skillet said it. Her hands said it in every motion.

If mornings were sacred, the rest of the day was sermon.

Work was not punishment in my grandmother's house. It was not something to dread or avoid. It was the rhythm that kept everything standing. She did not work with theatrics or sighs or the heavy performance of sacrifice. She worked because life required it, because families do not hold themselves together on their own, and because a house—especially one full of history—needed tending the way a garden needs water.

Clothes were washed by hand and wrung tight before being hung neatly across the line. Floors were swept not once but twice. Pots were scrubbed clean and set upside-down to dry. Sheets were shaken out in the yard, letting the sun bleach whatever life had stained. Every task had its proper place, its proper time, its proper motion.

Even her pauses had rhythm—never stops, only breaths. A sip of water. A moment in the doorway. A glance outside to check on the flowers or the chickens. Then back to the work that never complained.

As a child, I understood instinctively that everything she touched improved. The house was held together not by nails or boards but by her insistence that order could exist even in a world that rarely gave it. You could feel her everywhere—in the sheen on the wooden table, in the folded linens, in the faint smell of starch rising from the clothes she ironed with a steady, practiced hand.

The house breathed because she moved.

The house rested because she decided it could.

The house endured because she had.

Evenings came without ceremony. After supper, the house softened into itself. Dishes were dried and put away. Chairs were pushed back under the table. Windows were cracked just enough to let the night air in. Crickets took up their steady chorus outside, a sound so constant it felt like part of the walls.

I remember lying in bed listening—not for anything in particular, just listening. The house creaked and shifted the way living things do when they settle. Somewhere down the hall, my grandmother moved quietly, her presence known without needing to be seen.

Nothing happened. And because nothing happened, I slept.

By the time I entered the story, my older brother Will had already settled into the house as if he had been born into its quiet. Five years older than me, he carried extra seasons of her routines woven into him, seasons I would only glimpse through the way he moved through rooms and days.

Will knew when breakfast would be ready, when chores needed doing, when it was time to play and when it was time to come inside. He understood that the house ran on my grandmother's rhythm— and that her rhythm never wavered.

There was a softness in him then, shaped by the safety she gave him. He knew where his bed was, where his next meal was coming from, and that her voice—firm but never frantic—would call him in from the yard long before the streetlights came on.

Three years later, our little sister April would join us, the last child folded into my grandmother's care. She was younger, smaller, always trailing just behind—watching, listening, absorbing. If Will was my guide, April was my mirror: observant, sensitive, still soft around the edges in ways the rest of us had already hardened.

Origins

By the time April arrived, the house knew exactly how to make room. It had done it before.

I imagine myself then—small, carried through the doorway—unaware that the ground beneath me had held generations. Unaware that the hands lifting me were the same hands that had fed, disciplined, comforted, and buried children long before my name was ever spoken.

I did not know that other households felt different. I did not know instability existed elsewhere. I did not know the quiet I slept in had been earned through decades of noise, labor, sorrow, and prayer.

To me, the house had always been peaceful.

To my grandmother, it was peace she had earned.

I came into a world already living, into a house that had raised nearly an entire generation before I ever took my first step, into the care of a woman who had already lived multiple lifetimes.

This is where my story begins—

not at the beginning of the house,

but at the moment it opened its arms

and made room for me.

2

MY GRANDMOTHER'S HOUSE

Some of my earliest memories are of mornings spent outside with my grandmother, walking across the yard toward the chicken coop before the day had fully stretched awake.

The air was cool at that hour, soft against my skin, carrying the faint scent of dew and earth. She moved ahead of me with that familiar unhurried stride—steady, rhythmic, purposeful—her house shoes brushing lightly over the dirt as if she'd walked that same path her entire life.

The chickens recognized her long before they recognized me. They clucked and shifted at the sound of her approach, not in fear but in something close to greeting. She was the one who fed them, tended to them, gathered what they offered each morning. And I—small, following close behind—felt like I was being initiated into a private order of things.

She lifted the wooden door of the nesting box, and the warm smell of hay and feathers rose up like breath.

Origins

"Watch your fingers, gal," she murmured, her voice low and soft, wrapped in that East Texas cadence she never lost. She guided my hands to where the eggs rested—still warm, still holding the faintest trace of the hen's body heat.

To me, those eggs felt like magic. Life, cupped gently in my palms.

To her, it was simply work—daily, necessary, ordinary.

When we went back inside, she set the eggs on the counter and turned to the butter churn—an old wooden one with a handle smoothed by years of use. She lifted me onto a chair so I could see inside, then placed my hands over the handle, guiding them with hers.

"Steady," she said.

"Not fast. Just steady."

And I churned.

And churned.

And churned.

The sound of it—the soft slosh, the wooden plunger dipping through cream—taught me patience long before I knew the word. When the butter finally came together, she lifted it out with quiet satisfaction.

Homemade butter for homemade biscuits.

Nothing wasted.

Everything earned.

Even now, when I think of love, I think of her guiding my small hands—teaching me without explaining, shaping me without spectacle.

The yard behind my grandmother's house was its own small world. Beauty and danger lived side by side there without ever announcing themselves. To me, it felt endless—stretching past the chicken coop, past the flower beds she tended like living prayers, past the fig tree whose leaves cast shifting shadows across the ground.

Her flower nursery was the heart of it. Rows of blooms in old tubs, mismatched pots, beds carved straight into the soil. Neighbors stopped by to buy flowers or admire them, and my grandmother accepted praise with a nod. She knew the work. She didn't need applause.

One morning, when I was about seven, we were walking the familiar path along the fence line. Sunlight slanted through the trees. The earth smelled damp. Then—movement.

A snake.

Before I could react, my grandmother stepped forward, grabbed it by the tail, and swung it against the nearest tree.

One clean motion.

Final.

She didn't scream.

She didn't curse.

She didn't pray out loud.

She just kept walking. As if protecting children, chickens, and flowers from danger was simply another chore.

That was the moment I learned that gentleness and power are not opposites. They live in the same hands. The same woman who baked biscuits at dawn could face a threat without hesitation.

Inside the house, order continued without comment. Once, I tipped a glass of milk at the table. It spilled quickly, white spreading across the wood. I froze, waiting for the sound that never came. My grandmother stood, fetched a cloth, and wiped the mess without a word. When she finished, she looked at me—not angry, not indulgent—just steady.

"Pay attention next time," she said.

And that was all. The day continued.

My grandmother didn't speak often, but when she did, her words stayed. Her sayings were short, firm, shaped by years that had taught her not to waste breath.

"Yes ma'am, no ma'am—that's how you talk to grown folks."

"Everything that glitters is not gold."

"Once you get a man, you got yourself a problem."

Sometimes she would walk past a new baby and whisper,

"Goodness graces a life."

She'd say,

"I'll be there indirectly,"

and appear exactly when needed.

And when life surprised her, she'd exhale softly,

"I do declare…"

But what soothed me most was her singing; she had the most beautiful voice. Whenever we were restless or afraid, she would hum, low and steady:

This little light of mine,

KISCHA NICOL HERNANDEZ

I'm gonna let it shine...

She sang the way she lived—quietly, faithfully, without performance. Her voice always found me.

In that song, I felt safe.

In that song, I felt claimed.

For all its steadiness, my grandmother's house was not untouched by strain.

It sheltered us, but it could not keep the world from knocking.

3

MILLIE

My mother never entered a room quietly, even when she didn't say a word. She carried a presence that stirred the air—unsettling, unpredictable, alive in a way that felt foreign inside my grandmother's orderly house.

My grandmother's world ran on routine, calm, and discipline. Millie's world lived somewhere else entirely, and whenever she stepped into ours, the balance shifted.

I always knew when she was coming before anyone said so. Children learn to feel disruptions before they can name them. The energy tightened. My grandmother's movements grew sharper, more deliberate. Even the house seemed to brace—not out of fear, but out of experience.

Sometimes I knew she wasn't coming, but I waited anyway. I watched the road from the edge of the yard, kicking at the dirt, tracing shapes with my shoe. Each passing car made my stomach tighten, then release. When the dust settled and nothing followed, I went back inside without saying anything.

Waiting became something I did quietly.

And then Millie would appear.

She was beautiful in a way that felt troubled, like someone carrying stories she never learned how to lay down. Her eyes were sharp but tired; her body moved with the heaviness of someone who had lived too long without rest. Sometimes she arrived with laughter that didn't match the exhaustion in her face. Other times she came quiet, withdrawn, looking for a place to land that she knew she couldn't stay in.

Back then, I didn't understand addiction. I didn't understand trauma. I didn't understand why grown people could feel restless in their own skin. But I understood this:

when my mother came around,

something inside me went still.

She drifted in and out of the house like a visitor, even though she was my mother. Some days she brought gifts or promises or quick kisses. Other days she brought nothing at all, collapsing into my grandmother's bed and falling asleep almost immediately, as if she'd been fighting battles no one else could see.

She never stayed long enough to become part of the rhythm. She didn't fold into the routines the way the rest of us did. She hovered at the edges, landing briefly before drifting back into whatever life waited for her outside.

The first thing I remember about my mother wasn't her voice or her smile—it was her tiredness.

A deep, bone-level exhaustion that lived in her eyes and shoulders, in the way she exhaled as if the air inside her chest was always running low. She didn't walk into my grandmother's house like someone returning home. She walked in like someone seeking refuge—temporary, fragile, uncertain. Most of the time, she barely made it through the door before lying down. Couch. Bed. Wherever she landed. Sleep took her fast and hard, like a body surrendering.

She wasn't violent.

She wasn't cruel.

She wasn't loud.

She was just tired.

Sometimes she woke hours later and sat on the edge of the bed, smoothing her hair back with her palms like she was trying to gather herself. She'd look around the house as if orienting to a world that kept moving whether she was ready or not. Then she'd look at me—really look—and something in her expression softened.

In those moments, I caught a glimpse of the mother she might have been if life had given her something steadier. Her love came in fragments.

She would gently say my name—"Kischa... come here, baby"—and hold me near for a while. A kiss on my cheek. Fingers smoothing my braids. Sometimes she asked about school. Sometimes she just held me, warm and present for a few seconds before slipping away again.

She wasn't absent by choice.

She wasn't present by consistency.

She lived somewhere in between.

A mother who loved me, but couldn't raise me.

Who missed me, but couldn't stay.

I learned early to treasure what she gave without asking for more. Children adjust faster than adults realize. I adjusted to a love that arrived in brief sunlight through heavy clouds.

If Millie was the wind—restless, shifting, never still—then my grandmother was the ground beneath us. Firm. Unmoving.

My grandmother loved all her children, but she knew each one's limits. And when it came to Millie—the baby of her sixteen, born after so much heartbreak—she loved her fiercely without letting her unravel the world she had built. Her boundaries were not loud. They were lived.

When Millie arrived exhausted, my grandmother covered her with a blanket—but she did not indulge her chaos.

When Millie's temper rose, my grandmother cut it off with a single look.

When Millie drifted in and out of the house, my grandmother held the anchor steady without letting it drag the rest of us under.

"Now Millie... that'll do."

"Mind your ways while you're under my roof."

"The children don't need that here."

She didn't argue.

She didn't plead.

She simply stated what would and would not happen.

It wasn't hostility.

It was protection.

After my mother left, the house felt larger. Not emptier—just stretched. My grandmother moved through the rooms as she always did, unbothered, restoring order without comment. I followed her for a while, then drifted away, carrying a feeling I didn't know where to put.

By evening, the rhythm returned. It always did.

As a child, I didn't understand the dynamics. I only understood the feeling: when Millie appeared, I watched my grandmother take up her quiet authority—not with harshness, not with shame, but with the same steadiness she used to bake biscuits, tend flowers, or keep danger out of the yard.

She protected us.

Millie loved me and my siblings. There was never any doubt about that. But love alone could not steady her life—or mine.

My grandmother stepped in where my mother could not, becoming my anchor long before I had words for the shift.

Loving Millie was never the problem. Understanding her would come much later.

But surviving her absence required the protection of a stronger woman—and God had already placed that woman right beneath the same roof where I slept each night.

4

THE SILENCE THAT FOLLOWED

Some moments divide a childhood cleanly in two—before you knew, and after you knew.

For me, that moment came quietly. No warning. No ceremony. Delivered in a single sentence from my mother's mouth.

Millie came into my grandmother's house that day carrying a stillness I had never seen on her before. Not the exhaustion that usually weighed her down. Not the drifting haze that made her presence feel temporary. This was something else—focused, flat, emptied out.

She didn't collapse onto the bed. She didn't wander through the house. She came straight to me.

I was almost five.

Old enough to understand tone.

Too young to understand death.

She knelt down so we were eye to eye. Her face looked tired in a different way—hollowed, as if something had been scraped out of her. Her voice didn't tremble. It didn't soften. It didn't rise or fall.

"Kischa, your daddy's dead.

You won't see him again."

That was it.

No explanation.

No comfort.

No arms around me.

Just the truth, handed to me with the bluntness of someone who didn't have the strength to wrap it in anything gentler.

I didn't cry.

Not because I was brave—but because I did not understand.

Five-year-olds don't grasp finality. They grasp routine.

My father had been present in my life—loving, familiar in the small, ordinary ways children recognize as safety. His absence was noticeable long before its meaning was. No one explained murder to a child. No one told me how a life could be taken in an instant. No one told me how a man could disappear from the world without warning.

So I stood there quietly, holding words that had no shape yet, while the adults around me did what families of their generation often did in moments of trauma.

They went silent.

No one asked me what I felt.

No one explained what had happened.

No one told me what a child should do with a loss that large.

Maybe they thought I didn't understand.

Maybe they were trying to protect me.

Maybe they didn't have room for their own grief, much less mine.

But even at five, I felt the shift. Something in the world had tilted. Something foundational had been removed.

My father was gone.

And he was not coming back.

That afternoon, I ate when food was placed in front of me. I went outside when told. I came back in before dark. The day continued, stitched together by instruction and habit. If anyone noticed how carefully I followed the rules, they didn't say.

The world had changed.

The schedule had not.

Millie didn't stay long after she told me. She slipped away the way she always did, leaving behind the weight of words she couldn't carry herself. I never saw grief on her face—not the kind children expect to see.

Maybe she hid it.

Maybe it lived too deep.

Maybe she didn't know how to mother through sorrow when she couldn't mother through stability.

Years later, when I asked about my father, she told me he was handsome. That was the piece she held onto. Not the violence. Not the details. Just the beauty of the man she once loved.

Origins

I clung to that. A child will take any scrap of light when the world goes dim.

My grandmother's house did not change on the outside. Breakfast still sizzled in the skillet. Floors were swept. Flowers tended. Hymns hummed low. The routines remained intact, steady as ever.

But inside me, something shifted—and no one noticed.

Grief did not announce itself in our family. It settled quietly, unspoken, like dust in corners no one thought to check. The adults mourned through long stares, softer voices, sudden changes of subject.

And because they didn't speak, I didn't either.

Silence became the rule.

I learned to swallow questions before they reached my mouth.

I learned to tuck confusion away.

I learned to hold ache without naming it.

That night, I lay awake longer than usual. The house sounded the same as it always had—settled, breathing, intact. Somewhere down the hall, my grandmother moved once, then stopped. I closed my eyes and waited for sleep to take me where words could not.

My grandmother did not gather me into her arms and explain death. She did not kneel down and tell me everything would be all right. She did what she had always done when life demanded more than words could give.

She kept the house steady.

And she trusted that steadiness to hold me.

Looking back, I don't think anyone meant to teach me silence. It was simply the only language they had for grief. They had survived too much to unravel now.

So I grew up fluent in quiet.

In that quiet, I learned to observe.

In that quiet, I learned to endure.

In that quiet, the first version of my strength began to take shape—not loud, not angry, but inward, private, watchful.

If my grandmother's house shaped my body, and my mother shaped my questions, then my father's death shaped my silence.

This was the moment my childhood crossed from innocence into awareness—not because anyone guided me through it, but because no one did.

And in the spaces where words should have lived, silence became the language my life would learn to speak.

SERIES NOTE / WHAT COMES NEXT

This book is the first movement of the Raised by 1912™ series.

Book II, *Inheritance Without Permission*, continues the story—moving beyond the house and into the consequences of what was inherited, unspoken, and unresolved.

The silence does not end here.

IMPRINT PAGE

Storyhouse™ Publishing

Where legacy is written with care.

ACKNOWLEDGMENTS

This book was written in quiet gratitude

for those who held the line

without asking to be remembered.

ABOUT THE AUTHOR

Kischa Nicol Hernandez is a writer, attorney, and former investigator whose work centers on lineage, memory, and the quiet architecture of survival.

Raised in a multigenerational household shaped by discipline, routine, and silence, her writing explores the ways families transmit strength alongside unanswered questions. Raised by 1912™ is her debut memoir series.

She lives and works in Texas.

www.ingramcontent.com/pod-product-compliance
Lightning Source LLC
Chambersburg PA
CBHW031948070426
42453CB00007BA/509